CUSTOMS

Also by Solmaz Sharif

Look

CUSTOMS

Solmaz Sharif

Poems

Graywolf Press

This publication is made possible, in part, by the voters of Minnesota through a Minnesota State Arts Board Operating Support grant, thanks to a legislative appropriation from the arts and cultural heritage fund. Significant support has also been provided by Target Foundation, the McKnight Foundation, the Lannan Foundation, the Amazon Literary Partnership, and other generous contributions from foundations, corporations, and individuals. To these organizations and individuals we offer our heartfelt thanks.

Published by Graywolf Press
250 Third Avenue North, Suite 600
Minneapolis, Minnesota 55401

www.graywolfpress.org

Published in the United States of America

ISBN 978-1-64445-079-6

2 4 6 8 9 7 5 3 1
First Graywolf Printing, 2022

Library of Congress Control Number: 2021940564

Cover design and art: Mary Austin Speaker

for Afsaneh and Saeed

Contents

CUSTOMS

America

I had
to. I
learned it.
It was
if. If
was nice.
I said
sure. One
more thing.
One more
thing. Eat
it said.
It felt
good. I
was dead.
I learned
it. I
had to.

I

Dear Aleph,

Like Ovid: *I'll have no last words.*
This is what it means to die
among barbarians. *Bar bar bar*
was how the Greeks heard
our speech—sheep, beasts—and so we became
barbarians. We make them reveal
the brutes they are by the things
we make them name. David,
they tell me, is the one
one should aspire to, but ever since
I first heard them say *Philistine*
I've known I am Goliath
if I am anything.

Beauty

Frugal musicality is how Kristeva describes depression's speech

Cleaning out the sink drain

The melted cheese

The soggy muesli

My life can pass like this

Waiting for beauty

Tomorrow—I say

A life is a thing you have to start

The fridge is a thing with weak magnets, a little sweaty on the inside

A bag of shriveled limes

Arugula frozen then thawed then frozen again, still sealed

I haven't touched anyone in a year

You asked for beauty, and one morning, a small blue eggshell on the stoop, shattered open, its contents gone

Likely eaten

M asked if I've ever made a choice to live and why

I lied the way you lie to the suicidal

A few times, I said—not *Most days*

Most mornings

No, not morning

Morning I am still new

Still possible, I'm still *possibly*

Usually by 3:00

When grandmother died, she hadn't been called beautiful in at least half a century

Is never described as such

Her fallen stockings, the way she spit, thwack of the meat cleaver, the little bones she sucked clean and piled on her plate, not really looking at anything and certainly not me

Self-Care

Have you tried
rose hydrosol? Smoky quartz
in a steel bottle

of glacial water? Tincture
drawn from the stamens
of daylilies grown
on the western sides

of two-story homes?
Pancreas of toad?
Deodorant paste?

Have you removed
your metal fillings? Made peace
with your mother? With all
the mothers you can? Or tried

car exhaust? Holding your face
to the steaming kettle?
Primal screamed into

a down-alternative pillow
in a wood while tree-bathing?
Have you finally stopped
shoulding all over yourself?

Has your copay increased?
Right hip stiffened?
Has the shore risen

as you closed up the shop?
And have you put your weight
behind its glass door to keep
the ocean out? All of it?

Rang the singing bowl
next to the sloping toilet?
Mainlined lithium?

Colored in another mandala?
Have you looked
yourself in the mirror
and found the blessed halo

of a ring light in each iris?
Have you been content enough
being this content? Whose

shop was it?

Social Skills Training

Studies suggest *How may I help you officer?* is the single most disarming thing to say and not *What's the problem?* Studies suggest it's best the help reply *My pleasure* and not *No problem.* Studies suggest it's best not to mention *problem* in front of power even to say there is none. Gloria Steinem says women lose power as they age and yet the loudest voice in my head is my mother. Studies show the mother we have in mind isn't the mother that exists. Mine says: *What the fuck are you crying for?* Studies show the baby monkey will pick the fake monkey with fake fur over the furless wire monkey with milk, without contest. Studies show to negate something is to think it anyway. *I'm not sad.* I'm not sad. Studies recommend regular expressions of gratitude and internal check-ins. *Enough*, the wire mother says. History is a kind of study. History says we forgave the executioner. Before we mopped the blood we asked: *Lord Judge, have I executed well?* Studies suggest yes. *What the fuck are you crying for, officer?* the wire mother teaches me to say, while studies suggest *Solmaz, have you thanked your executioner today?*

Dear Aleph,

You're correct. Every nation hates
its children. This is a requirement of statehood.

This and empathy.
Empathy means

laying yourself down
in someone else's chalklines

and snapping a photo. A Chrysler
with four bullet holes

in the rear passenger door
just drove by calmly, signaling

before it turned. *Oh, Mrs. Evans,
you're such a wonderful woman,*

said, supposedly, Ethel Rosenberg
to the woman who walked her

to the chair.
It was empathy on Evans's part.

Love on Ethel's.
I am a wonderful woman

more often than I care to admit.
We are going to have

our first woman president.

Visa

From past participle of *videre* or *to see*.

The sight decided by officer.

The officer deciding by blood sugar, last blow job received, and
    relative level of disdain for vermin.

Domestic terminals do not have this railing at the exit.

As we wait for her to exit customs, our sightline is obstructed
    by opaque sliding doors, the twisting hallway behind it, the
    small convex mirror hung in the corner in which we catch
    shapes growing larger, into hair color, into gait, into age, and
    finally, as they turn, into kin.

The hours I've stood there, behind that railing.

The hours I've stood to savor the seconds earlier, seconds more
    by which my eye may reach the disembarking and exclaimed,
    She's here, watched, from shadow to shape to gait, my
    imagined life come to life and approach, briefly, me.

My imagined life crying hot in my ear.

Ink on its fingerpads.

This will be the last I write of it directly, I say each time.

This is a light that lights everything and dimly.

All my waiting at this railing.

All my writing is this squint.

Persistence of Vision: Gwendolyn Brooks

In the rearview, fog extinguishes the hills of new
money—mansions on acres away from road or sight.
Their architected privacy, windows to look out at
a land that won't look back. The fog's secure drapery.
It's space to dance through they buy and what one
might call "dappled light" moving across their acres, light
through their oaks moving over their mares, brushed to a sheen.

Palms of sugar cubes. Soft snorting, I bet. Here, Muybridge
proved their horses fly a moment. In their homes, they can't
hear each other call from foyer to pool house. I am
jealous of this loneliness most of all—loneliness
delimited by colonnade and cold-pressed juices.
*They make excellent corpses, among the expensive
flowers.* . . . I imagine hills and hills dappled like this.

Planetarium

sign reading CHOOSE LIFE
sign reading SOLVE THE WATER CRISIS
sign reading WARNING: UNEXPLODED SHELLS
sign reading DATE SHAKES
which does not mean as we guess
shaking the palm trees until the dates fall
but what comes out of a blender
We are like aliens we say
and can you believe our luck when out
to watch the stars the Joshua Tree dark
interrupted by a boom that is not thunder
a flash that is not lightning from over
the low nearby mountain
but is of course the air force base
running tests or training or regardless
I wanted to write about stars for once and looking
at them thought *My God* thought
This is just like a planetarium
thought of the glow in the dark stars
I stuck all over my bedroom
when between the explosions
it was dark enough

Now What

And so I sat at a tall table
in an Ohio hotel,
eating delivery:
cheese bread

with garlic butter, only it was
not butter, but partially
hydrogenated soy-
bean oil

and regular soybean oil and it
came in a little tub like
creamer that's also not
dairy.

America in this century
means a poem will have to
contain dairy that is,
in fact,

not dairy. On Instagram: a man
has bought a ten-foot-by-four-
foot photo of a bridge
he lives

beside, bridge he can see just outside
his window, window which serves
as a ten-foot-by-four-
foot frame.

My materialist mind, I can't
shake it. Within a perfect
little tub of garlic
butter,

a relief of workers, of sickles,
fields of soy. We were tanners
pushed to the edge of the
city

once, by the stench, the bubble of vats
of flesh and loosening skin,
back when the city pulled,
leather

bucket by leather bucket, its own
water from wells. Then we worked
the cafeterias
at the

petroleum offices of the
British. Then, revolution.

Simple.

Persistence of Vision: Televised Confession

You are like a daughter
to me—the prisoner's
mother tells me. Meal by
meal she sets then clears. She

rinses some tableware
the prisoner never
held, then a glass she did,
then recalls her daughter's

mouth opening softly
to drink water on state-
run TV, then water
over everything. The

glass appears in hundreds
of frames before reaching
the prisoner's lips. In
between each frame, the grief

our eyes jump to create
movement: dark strips to keep
sharp the glass lip, water
skin trembling, hand that

trembles it. These mothers
move as flipbooks, tiny,
stuttering pasts, sobbing
at the sink. It is death

that sharpens our sight each
sixteenth second, slender,
blocking enough light so
that the prisoner's face

is again and again
alive each light-punctured
frame, her mouth, in hundreds
of stills, is still opening

softly to drink.

He, Too

Upon my return to the US, he
asks my occupation. Teacher.

What do you teach?
Poetry.

I hate poetry, the officer says,
I only like writing
where you can make an argument.

Anything he asks, I must answer.
This, too, he likes.

I don't tell him
he will be in a poem
where the argument will be

anti-American.

I place him here, puffy,
pink, ringed in plexi, pleased

with his own wit
and spittle. Saving the argument
I am let in

I am let in until

Dear Aleph,

I've arrived
frilled. Laced.
Softly etched.

Tomato juice on Carrara marble,
the ruin of it.
The training of the eye

only wealth can—
only wealth can
ruin one's sight like this.

Only gout, plucked
pheasant, &c.
I tried to quell or quiet

my bile, but it grew
horns instead.
In the basement, it fed

from the steel bowl,
the congealed and cold
cartilage left,

and now I can confess,
there is nothing to them:
the Americans.

Not élan, quiddity.
A hateful people,
as all, and easy

to offend.
Send word, you said.
The line frays.

It is of love
I say this. It is of love,
I must say,

but not of thee.

Learning Persian

deek-teh
deek-tah-tor
behn-zeen
dee-seh-pleen
eh-pe-deh-mi
fahn-te-zi
mu-zik
bahnk
mah-de-mah-zel
sees-tem
tah-ahtre
vah-nil
vee-la
vee-roos
ahm-pee-ree-ah-lizm
doh-see-eh
oh-toh-ree-te

Patronage

They say
willingness is what one needs
to succeed.

They say one needs to succeed.

•

Our poets do not imagine
a screaming

audience.

Our poets are used to padding,

vinyl, on the foldable chairs,
bookshelves on casters
moved aside
to make space for them.

A world polite
for their words.

A well-behaved.
A world's behavior

malformed and they step
in as one steps in
to a nursery and

quiet

calms the tantrum,
attempts not to wake
the sleeping, the milk-drunk

and burped babe.

Our poets coo.

And beg to be placed in a large room.

•

Prize ring. Bull ring. Lion
through the ring of flames.

Poets convinced they are ringmaster
when it is with big brooms and bins, in fact,
they enter to clear the elephant scat.

•

There was an inlet.
I pulled over once to watch the sunset, which
was still another hour or so away, the light
just low enough there to begin to change.
I should've stayed. I should've stayed.

•

A life of idle, with money

doing the work. A life beholden,
but bestowed. To make reformists of us all,

even the fascists.
       Especially

the fascists.

    •

But he's a patron.
But he makes a star of us,
he makes us of rank.

But he's a churchgoer

and they place their hands on him and pray and bountiful
grow their wives' bellies, a bully
for each family. Exponential doom.

Singing to each other in the private gazebo of their youth.

    •

Now sing.

    •

I said what I meant
but I said it

in velvet. I said it in feathers.
And so one poet reminded me,

Remember what you are to them.

Poodle, I said.

And remember what they are to you.

•

Meat.

Into English

I think I will translate
Forough.
I am urged to translate
Forough

as soon as possible.
In my
hours, I find it is
very

private. It is very
private
to be in another's
syntax.

Look! a translator holds
up for
the flash, a hooked and
thrashing

bass. *Lament. Lament,* an-
other
says. I say let them have
it: the

think-tank wonks, the panty-
sniffing
critics, the consultant
for the

US Navy. Noble,
they call
it. These saviors into
English.

She asked a friend to bring her a window and a lamp
I ask a friend to bring me a window and a lamp
We watch the thronging, lucky alley
We wave to each other not

Who would I do it for?
You? I
have forgotten even
myself

as reader. I turn off
our light.

The End of Exile

As the dead, so I come
to the city I am of.
Am without.

To watch play out around me
as theater —

audience as the dead are audience

to the life that is not mine.
Is as not
as never.

Turning down Shiraz's streets
it turns out to be such

a faraway thing.

A without which
I have learned to be.

From bed, I hear a man in the alley
selling something, no longer by mule and holler
but by bullhorn and jalopy.

How to say what he is selling —

it is no thing
this language thought worth naming.
No thing I have used before.

It is his
life I don't see daily.
Not theater. Not play.

Though I remain only audience.

It is a thing he must sell daily
and every day he peddles

this thing: a without which

I cannot name.

Without which is my life.

II

Without Which

]]

I have long loved what one can carry.
I have long left all that can be left
behind in the burning cities and lost

even loss—not cared much
or learned to. I turned and looked
and not even salt did I become.

]]

]]

I have long not wanted much
touch to turn away from and sleep
a sleep to bring the spoon up
and slurp the soup I don't notice gone.

Like that mostly, my life.

　　]]

Until I see something new.

It does not happen much.

Except in the sense that everything is new.

　　]]

Three baby teeth in a washed-clean, baby-food jar
rattling

as the drawer opens and closes or

the train passes underneath
or our bed bumps into the nightstand,

　　]]

into the wall,
sliding across the room,

chattering loose teeth I wanted to hold on to
in a glass jar for what? for how long?

Eventually I pare down

      ]]

what of me I can't stand to look at,

what of me I'd never want recognized,

by whoever will clear out my drawers,
whoever does such a thing at the end
of a life,

      ]]

who years wanted nothing,

who was dead before she died.

      ]]

]]

]]

]]

Before you came, I hadn't touched another
in years. It was unintentional.
Frugal.

Later and the satisfaction of a small life

closed in a single mind.

   ]]

Your thin drawer.

Pocket squares folded into neat stacks.
Wristwatches laid flat into neat—

You looked at me
looking at your things.

   ]]

I touched the satin squares.

I touched the satin scar
where you had been cut.

   ]]

Your healthy walking.
Your wristwatch removed

and ticking in this room.

To watch you
get dressed while still in bed

      ]]

is a little city where
I'm most grateful to be alive, gently

ticking—naked, leisurely
watching a slightly warped record

turn, its tiny hills

      ]]

raising the needle, too, gently.

      ]]

]]

]]

Of
is such a little city

]]

and can hold only so much.

Of is the thing without which
I would not be.

        ]]

Of which I am without
or away from.
I am without the kingdom

        ]]

and thus of it.

I am—
even when inside the kingdom—

without.

        ]]

Smelling the dried dill,
the day-old, slick fish—

even my hems wet
with the gutters of the kingdom

I am of—

      ]]

even so
more so

out of it.

      ]]

A without which
I have learned to be.

      ]]

And *I am forgotten as a dead man out of mind.*

A static crackling.

    ]]

I pointed to his two unwaxed shoes,
their torn laces, and asked,

Have you worn them long?

Hardly ever, he said.
On his wrist,

    ]]

a dead man's watch.

In his pockets, dates
he had pulled from the palm

at the end of the block,

    ]]

palm bent
to the street
by a tank. He,

thin as a second hand,

looks at whatever I look at.

]]

This door, for now,

with half-moons
of paint scraped

away by the swinging
knockers.

]]

Door I would have answered—

here is the *might have*

]]

otherwise been

just before it is razed.
Here is the home

as far as from
can go.

]]

Would you have knocked for me?
I ask the neighbor.

I have been, he said.

Then I felt his knocking

]]

inside my chest.

]]

]]

]]

]]

On the edges of the cities,
our boiling vats—

The tanneries do not smell good.

]]

Did not:

the skins boiled to loosen the flesh,
to pull clean

what will be

]]

leather, be
bucket
to lower in a well.

Out around the edge
of the city

]]

is where you would
find the tanners,
pushed there by rot.

We who at the edge
of the kingdom

    ]]

pulled dead from dead
to sculpt
the simplest, repeated thing
now obsolete:

leather buckets

    ]]

to pull up out of the dark
a cool, shimmering surface
to see yourself in

    ]]

—one single, shimmering eye.

]]

This glimpse of myself, bucket
by bucket,
is what I am missing.

]]

]]

The crumbs have been swept
from the tables, shaken from the skirts,
the dates returned to their containers,
the last of the mourners gone.

Homeland is where one's wake was held
and so—

                ]]

No crueler word than *return*.
No greater lie.

The gates may open but to *return*.
More gates were built inside.

                ]]

                ]]

I've learned the sound
of nestlings being fed, their mad
chirping now clear in the trees
I walk beneath. There are languages

I didn't know I wanted
to know.

]]

I've learned the sound of jets
over Oakland for Fleet Week.

]]

Something about a nest.
Something about a tree
scared bald and shaken free
so all its empty nests

are exposed.
Something about my neural pathways like that.

]]

Like, I've decided,

is the cruelest word.

To step out of my door and hope to see
something like a life,
something passably me,

]]

like the cage of canaries baba put out
to sun in the Shiraz courtyard, the birds
dropping dead onto the shit-covered newsprint
when a cat slunk by.

]]

I prayed for the smallest happiness
today, a pool of water
in an Oakland pothole,

]]

a single likeness to see
feathers lifting, then shaking free,

then something like a cat I became
to frighten dead any hopeful thing.

    ]]

Some days, I am almost happy having never
lived there.

To lose even the loss.

    ]]

    ]]

]]

]]

Some days,
                just to think

of washing some dishes—
mismatched and in a rust-stained sink—

touching things I have spent my whole life

]]

touching—

]]

]]

]]

The Master's House

To wave from the porch
To let go of the grudge
To disrobe
To recall Ethel Rosenberg's green polka-dotted dress
To call your father and say, *I'd forgotten how nice everyone in these
     red states can be*
To hear him say, *Yes, long as you don't move in next door*
To recall every drawn curtain in the apartments you have lived
To find yourself at thirty-three at a vast expanse with nary a
     papyrus of guidance, with nary a voice, a muse, a model
To finally admit out loud then, *I want to go home*
To have a dinner party of intellectuals with a bell, long-armed,
     lightly-tongued, at each setting
To sport your dun gown
To revel in face serums
To be a well-calibrated burn victim to fight the signs of aging
To assure financial health
To be lavender sachets and cedar lining and all the ways the rich
     might hide their rot
To eye the master's bone china
To pour diuretic in his coffee and think this erosive to the state
To disrobe when the agent asks you to
To find a spot on any wall to stare into
To develop the ability to leave an entire nation thusly, just by
     staring at a spot on the wall, as the lead-vested agent names
     article by article what to remove
To do this in order to do the other thing, the wild thing
To say this is my filmdom, The Master's House, and I gaze upon
     it and it is good
To discuss desalination plants and terroir
To date briefly a banker, a lapsed Marxist, and hear him on the
     phone speaking in billions of dollars, its residue over the clear
     bulbs of his eyes, as he turns to look upon your nudity

To fantasize publishing a poem in the *New Yorker* eviscerating his little need

To set a bell at each intellectual's table setting ringing idea after idea, and be the simple-footed help, rushing to say, *Yes?*

To disrobe when the agent asks you to

To find a spot on any wall to stare into

To develop the ability to leave an entire nation thusly, just by staring at a spot on the wall

To say this is my filmdom, The Master's House

To recall the Settler who from behind his mobile phone said, *I'm filming you for God*

To recall this sad God, God of the mobile phone camera, God of the small black globe and pixelated eye above the blackjack table at Harrah's and the metal, toothed pit of Qalandia checkpoint the same

To recall the Texan that held a shotgun to your father's chest, sending him falling backward, pleading, and the words came to him in Farsi

To be jealous of this, his most desperate language

To lament the fact of your lamentations in English, English being your first defeat

To finally admit out loud then, *I want to go home*

To stand outside your grandmother's house

To know, for example, that in Farsi the present perfect is called the relational past, and is used at times to describe a historic event whose effect is still relevant today, transcending the past

To say, for example, *Shah dictator bude-ast* translates to *The Shah was a dictator*, but more literally to *The Shah is-was a dictator*

To have a tense of is-was, the residue of it over the clear bulb of your eyes

To walk cemetery after cemetery in these States and nary a gravestone reading *Solmaz*

To know no nation will be home until one does

To do this in order to do the other thing, the wild thing, though you've forgotten what it was

III

Does yours have a landscape?

—Yes.

Because mine has a landscape.

—It is a path of small and sharp stone and it is lined with cypresses.

And are there other paths that you are aware of?

—One for each of us.

And are you waving?

—We will never see each other.

And are you aware of the waving?

An Otherwise

Downwind from a British Petroleum refinery, my mother is removing the books she was ordered to remove from the school library. Russians, mostly. Gorky's *Mother* among them. The Shah is coming to tour the school. It is winter.

In the cold, the schoolgirls line up along the front of the main building and wait for his motorcade. Knee-highs and pleated skirts. Shivering in the refined air.

Wave, girls, the teacher says.

My mother, waving.

Put another way:
The must of the glued
spines and silverfish, metal
shelves, my mother

reaching by tiptoe
to take down Gorky,
for example,

filling her arms
with stacks of books.
The Dickens could stay.
You understand.

And the air is important to note
for what it is doing
to the pink

lungs, bronchioles—
a life of inflammation.
Wave, girls, the teacher says
to the shivering

and ironed line of them.
And wave she did.
And if he cared

to see
into the minds of teenaged girls,
this King
would've seen then

the rifles pointed at him.

When I was a small child,
I think, about five or six, greatness
didn't touch me—lifted

her hems walking through
my hall. A set of colorful magnets
made an incomplete alphabet.

Gouges in the chalkboard
on my lap, chalkless. Someone
put it there and closed the door

to answer the phone.
The news
came, terrific.

Someone howling, *No*—

The news was greatness.

Another way yet:
Fuck the British.
The Soviets.
The Shah and the righteous

air of her life.
And bless the lung,
the sensitive bronchioles,

the filigree of finite health,
and her singing
at the foot of my bed,
over the sink,

in the Istanbul restaurant where a young waiter
rests his tray and cries
into his sleeve.

When I was a small child,
I think, about five or six, I must've
heard something, some cassette turning

to dust in the car's player,
notes stretched, song
that quieted, in the front seat,

my parents, some tape spooled back
with a ballpoint pen and worn
to mica in the car's player as the turn signal

clicked its quiet, and the keys
clicked with the wide and final turn—
song which was, I'm sure,

an ancient poem sung and filled
with cypresses, their upright
windscreen for what must be grown.

Downwind, I walked the wide hallways
of a great endowment.

It didn't matter if I did or didn't.
It changed only myself, the doing.

It fed down to one knuckle
then the next, this compromise.

It fed down to one frequency
and another, leaving me only a scrambled sound.

It would burn your fingertips
to walk the length of the hall

dragging them along the grass-papered walls
where they punished you

for not
wanting enough. For not wanting

to be nonbelligerent
by naming the terms

for belligerence.
The shellacked

shelves, the softly shaking
pens in their pencase.

What was given there
could be taken, and

quietly, you were reminded of this.
You were reminded all

was property of the West.
The mess of a raven's nest

built behind a donor's great bust
then gone.

The mess of bird shit on the steps
then gone. All dismantled and scrubbed

sensibility. And this was it.
This nowhere.

My school of resentment commenced.

What I meant to say:
the thing killed: little
furred creature crouched
and licking clean

its hindquarters in peaceful
huddle found in the back
of my dumb heart. When I went

I found nothing.
It died there: desire.
All fantasy
of return.

Caravan gone, fire smoldering.
Nights
were longer

with you in them.
Private solstice.
One who laid back,

kingly,
hands beneath his head,
elbows wide

to wait for what
will be done
to him.

One who said the poem was
not fair.
It was not.

One I needed to destroy.
One to humiliate.
One against whose door

I knocked, still knock
to be let in, beloved.
This is the oldest poem

the older poet said,
outside the door of the beloved
asking to be let in—

Alluring otherwise life.
Life without exchange rate.

Life where what is
is. Simply.

Long down the back of the throat.
Root noise.

Speaking to its own.
Answering the mewing

at the closed doors.

What awaits us on the other side
of alphabet,
scrawl

serrated, all slit,
all hole,

red with scream,
I do not know.

The knowing is the dullest part of all.

Someone posts a picture of the Poet's tomb
and I want to say,
That's my city—

but I am left with the lie of *my*.
I said what I said and stayed
saying

what I came to say

long after the people left.
A poet as a fixed position

most cannot stand to be in
for long.

Someone snaps a photo and moves on.
Someone provides a corpse for this great wall.

Maybe I shouldn't have taken you there,
she said of our trip
to her childhood home.
For years I wrote of the bumps

left by the tanks
churning over her roads
as *braille messages from the martyrs,*

which meant I missed
it entirely,
the only
it:

my mother's face
turned out
the passenger window,

just looking.

What did you leave behind?
We answered:

A pool
lined

with evergreens,
needles falling

into water,
its floor

painted milky
jade. A car

in the driveway.
A mother.

Another mother.
A cockatiel

in the hallway
squawking

next to the plastic
slippers.

Glass
after beveled glass.

Secret
after beveled secret.

Letters
from a first

crush
now dead.

Killed.
We wanted

to be asked
of these things.

To tell of them
was to live

again. We spent
much of our lives

imagining.
We rathered

and rathered,
scraping the soft

moss
off

the gravestones
of our early

curiosities.

Summer. Harvest done.
The last stone fruit

pitted, jarred,
spoiling the last white shirt—

Row of cypress,
sun-blistered

fences.
Solid and settled masonry.

The unseen town
and town just

beyond.
The echo

as if inside
a room of stone.

I felt each world
was one cypress-lined path

and each path had
one of us, bagless

and awake, walking
wind and footfalls.

I felt we were heading
to meet somewhere.

I tried to say it was dead, the song,
but then it came, my mother singing
of cypress—

I tried to leave the literal,
but it got lonely—

I tried to leave desire,
but it scratched at the door, tapped
its empty bowl against the floor—

I tried not to answer,
but the bulb shone—

And I saw that the head bent over
a book I couldn't see
beneath a single yellow lamp

through the evening window

of a childhood not mine
was my mother's
mind alight

learning to oil a rifle.

The astrologer asks if I've done
the ancestral work because

It is hard to tell, she says,
what is meant for you—it's crowded
here. She feels,

to me,

eager to leave.
Seems still to believe

it possible, the uncontaminated,
as if it were ever I

talking to her
or ever she—

And though when they first
appeared, I didn't know, I am reminded
a sprig

of cypress hung
meant death happened here.

It seemed she might back away
from the stench—

There are too many and it is hard
to tell what is for you
in the noise.

I didn't ask if the prisoner
with the sharpened spoon handle
to the wrist

came, saying, *Tell my mother*—
or the mother

salting a meal she won't taste herself.
At a gate, it seemed

the officers knew I was coming.
Their questions tailored.

At a gate, I was asked
the name of my father,

my father's father,
beneath a shivering bulb,

and whether I write
plays.

At a gate, one man
selling gladiolas

wrapped in plastic
out of a black bucket.

One selling wreaths.
One selling water.

At a gate, the men gathered to discuss
building

a playground
over the unmarked graves.

At a gate, I watched one hand
outstretched saying,

Come.
I thought it was loss—

language, its little
radius—

when it's a beckoning,
a way.

At one gate, my mother waving.

Enough, I said.
I plotted.
In the mornings, I wrote.

In my sleep, I wrote
with fancier, more elaborate inks.
And in my writing, I began to write of cypresses.

And of small and sharp stone.
And I, on this path, a wooden handle in my palm, and a blade
    at the end of it.
And beyond, their windscreen, the unseen.

I knew not the poem, only the weather.
I knew not the listening, only this landscape, its one clear channel.

The metal in my teeth caught its frequency.
The iron shavings of my blood pulled toward this otherwise.

And so upon that path
without obvious company,

I set out, as she set out,
armed, later than I would

like, to follow
the music mine

and not, but matrilineal,
and in the amniotic sac

of sound
reaching where the listening

ends and the mind alights,
in that dim red glow,

I wipe clean my blade
I tap at the door

I pass through there so that

Acknowledgments

Thank you to the following publications for publishing earlier versions of poems in this collection: Academy of American Poets' *Poem-a-Day*, *Deadlines and Divine Distractions*, *Freeman's*, *Granta*, *Harper's Magazine*, the *Paris Review*, *Poetry*, *Social Text*, and the *Yale Review*.

Thank you to the Lannan Foundation, MacDowell, the Radcliffe Institute, and Stanford University, for the incubation. Thank you to Arizona State University and all my colleagues.

Thank you to Jeff Shotts and his green path, Chantz Erolin, and all at Graywolf.

Thank you, rafiqs, for the conversations and calls about the poems in here and the air around them: Ari Banias, Luis Bocaletti, Jos Charles, Arash Davari, Natalie Diaz, Adam Fitzgerald, Fady Joudah, Shoaib Kamil, Rickey Laurentiis, Golnar Nikpour, Maisha Quint, marcos ramirez, Roger Reeves, Margaret Ross, Charif Shanahan, Safiya Sinclair, Wendy Trevino, and Samira Yamin.

Thank you, Eavan.

And thank you to my parents, Afsaneh and Saeed.

Thank you, fear. That's enough now.

SOLMAZ SHARIF is the author of *Look*, a finalist for the National Book Award. She is currently an assistant professor at Arizona State University where she is inaugurating a Poetry for the People program.

The text of *Customs* is set in Adobe Garamond Pro.
Book design by Rachel Holscher.
Composition by Bookmobile Design and Digital
Publisher Services, Minneapolis, Minnesota.
Manufactured by Versa Press on acid-free,
30 percent postconsumer wastepaper.